Ma  Storage Auctions: How to Profit from the Storage Wars and become a Storage Auction Warrior

Copyright © 2011 by Boston Reynolds
All rights reserved. This book or any portion thereof may not be reproduced or used in any manner whatsoever without the express written permission of the publisher except for the use of brief quotations in a book review.

Printed in the United States of America

First Printing, 2011

Preface

Making money from buying storage lockers at auction is a booming trend. It's possible to work only a few hours per day and still make a big time profit.

Buying items for resale at storage auctions is a great way to make money. Depending on the auction, you can be bidding on something as small as a single box or carton, to as large as an entire 400 square foot storage room. What you are doing is buying the entire contents at a wholesale price, and expecting that the merchandise you find inside will allow you to double or triple your investment, or more. The storage company has a problem; they have a unit that's full of stuff that they need to remove. You get to buy this stuff at a steep discount, throwing some out, and reselling the rest for a tidy sum of money.

While it is possible to make a good amount of money this way, there are also risks of which you should be aware. Lots of different things can be found in this units, and you almost never get to inspect what's inside before you buy them. You might get stuck with a bunch of old rags, or a few moldy mattresses. Or worse, you can have a huge volume of goods, but that have no resale value whatsoever.

So how do you take advantage of the profit potential that these auctions present without losing your shirt? This book will give you tips and strategies about the process, and how to maximize your return while minimizing risk. We will also go over the procedures and rules, so that you can avoid common mistakes in the process. And, we'll give an example of an easy to follow system for selecting items to buy, how to organize yourself and your team, and some tips on how and where to resell your purchase for maximum profit.

Storage auctions are a great opportunity to make money by helping everyone out. Let's get started!

Contents

Preface 3

Introduction 7

Chapter One: Storage Auctions 11

    What kind of return should I try to get? 13

    How much can you make? 14

    The Value of Research 16

    Doing Research at the Auction Itself 18

    What's that smell? 22

    What you may hope to find, and what you may actually find 23

    Tips for Bidding on Units 26

    Choose wisely 27

    Common Mistakes 29

    What not to do 32

Chapter Two: Running the Business 35

    Locating Auctions 36

    Creating Your Own Auction Calendar 38

    Figuring out how much stuff is worth 38

    Deciding what to keep and what to throw away 40

    Dealing With Trash 41

    Keeping a Selling Calendar 45

    Having enough cash 46

- Have Transportation 47
- Having people to help 49
- Having a place to put all the items 51
- Chapter Three: Reselling...53
  - Tips for Reselling 54
  - Before you sell 55
  - Selling immediately...56
  - Flea Markets 58
  - Selling at Yard Sales 60
  - Selling to a pawn shop 61
  - Selling your items on eBay.......................................62
  - Selling on Craigslist 64
  - Selling online...66

Introduction

So, what exactly is a storage auction?

Across the country, there are thousands of businesses usually known as mini-storage centers. This is a place where people, usually for a monthly fee, can keep a large variety of things that either don't fit into their current living space, or that they don't use frequently, and simply want out of their house. This can range from old photos, to excess furniture, gold coins or grandma's china. It can also contain things like old clothes, or even trash. It's a great business to be in, all you need to do is own a building, carve up some spaces, provide locks, and charge a monthly fee. Of course, like any other business, there are people who don't pay their bills, or walk away leaving you holding the bag (in this case, possibly literally.) When this happens, the Storage Center is authorized to sell the goods that are inside at auction, and use the money raised to defray the back rent owed on the unit.

There is a lot of information to know about storage auctions, and we will try to cover as many possible in this book. We will talk about how the auction process works, how you get to participate, what types of items you are likely to find, and other questions. Of course, the landscape is ever changing, and new resources will be popping up every day, and some others will disappear. This book will do its best to remain current.

Okay, so a storage unit gets put up for auction when the renter of the unit is behind on their bill. States vary as to how late a person can be, but the average is between three and six months. The storage company is obligated to do everything in their power to get the person to pay their bill, right up until the morning of the auction itself. However, there comes a time when they've exhausted all possible avenues, and it's time for them to figure out a way to minimize their losses.

The process of holding a storage auction varies from state to state and company to company. Some states place very strict guidelines on the storage company with regards to how long they have to wait, how many times they have to try to contact the owner, etc. Some companies have very strict rules, others are more flexible, it really depends on the storage unit owner and the company holding the auction. In fact, it's quite common for the company holding the auction to be a third-party that specializes in storage auctions, and not the unit company itself. Most often, you are bidding on an entire unit and everything in it. It is possible to go to a "container" auction, however, where you are bidding on one or more boxes at a time. Conceptually, these are not different from each other, so we'll consider them the same for our purposes.

The amazing thing about these auctions is what you can find there. You can really find just about anything from jewelry to cars, furniture to old holiday decorations. The things that are put in storage are things that the owner didn't have room to keep themselves, but are too valuable to just throw away. In fact, the owner was paying rent so as not to have to throw these items away! Of course, you don't know what you are getting before you buy it; most places don't let you inspect the items any more than looking into the unit from the outside. Many times, you are buying a sealed box, and it's a mystery what is inside.

Anyone can participate in these auctions; they are open to the public. Some states require a small fee if you don't have a reseller's license, but this isn't common. Everyone wants the bidding to get as high as possible by encouraging participation. If there is a fee, it is usually very small. Really all you need to start bidding is identification and cash.

There are lots of reasons people participate in these auctions. People who love going to yard sales will also love the storage auction world. Anyone looking to buy lots of items cheaply will also do well. But mostly, people are there to buy items that they will resell elsewhere. We'll cover reselling later in the book.

Storage auctions are the result of the owner not wanting to throw things out, but then defaulting on the rental agreement they signed. Anyone can participate and buy the items at auction, and the auctions are fairly easy to find. Once you get the hang of it, you can find units to buy that contain items you can resell for a handy profit.

Let's get started!

Chapter One: Storage Auctions

In our current environment, many people have fallen behind on paying their bills and obligations. One of the bills that people are finding it easy not to pay is the rent on their storage unit. It's not as if they are living in the unit, and they have been living without the items that are in there for quite a while as it is. We, as a nation, are excellent consumers and purchasers, but not nearly as effective at saving. Lots of us have bought many things that we don't really need, even expensive things, and never used them. These kinds of things can wind up in storage units, along with keepsakes, valuable collectables, and a myriad of other possessions.

After some number of months, and the number is different in each state, the storage unit company has the right to try to recoup some of its losses by selling the goods within at auction. This is where we come in. We buy other people's goods at a huge discount, and resell them to people who want them for a profit. It's not only totally legal, it is encouraged by all involved. The storage company gets a clean locker, the original owner gets forgiven their debt, and you get lots of great stuff for very little cost.

As we move deeper into the 21st century, people are looking to add to their sources of income. The stock market is unreliable, jobs are unpredictable, and everything is unstable. Being the owner of your own business, controlling your own destiny, has a certain appeal to millions of Americans. Buying items at auction can give you a steady income, and a good return on your investment. Not only that, you are buying tangible goods, in fact, goods that someone once purchased for themselves. That means that they almost certainly have intrinsic value, which lowers your risk. At the very least, if you buy a bureau that you cannot sell, you can use it yourself. If you are buying actual assets, it is very difficult for you to lose all of your investment.

So, if you've been looking for a way to make extra money without working another job, or having to make minimum wage at a menial task, then being a storage auction buyer may be for you. You don't need any special education or license, you probably don't need a lot of cash to get started, and really, the only thing you need is a pickup truck – or a friend who has one.

Being a buyer of storage units is also something that you can do part time, while you keep your day job. It's a fun experience to do with your spouse, or your kids, or your brothers and sisters. You can control when and how often you work, thought the harder you work, the more you'll make. There are very few business opportunities where you get this kind of flexibility, with this kind of expected return on your money.

What kind of return should I try to get?

A good rule of thumb, and to know if you are doing well, is to try to make between a 50 and 75% return on your investment. This means that for every $100 you spend, you should be trying to get back $150 to $175. This isn't that difficult to do, but it requires you understanding how to estimate the value of the contents of a unit, and to understand the auction mentality. There is also an element of luck involved, as you aren't usually able to examine the goods you are about to purchase, and you can sometimes be surprised at what you find. Sometimes, you'll find items of much more than expected value inside, sometimes it'll be less. Attempting to average 50 to 75% is realistic, though sometimes you'll make much more, while other times you'll make less.

Of course, as with any business, you'll have expenses. You'll have to have transportation, you'll may have to hire someone (or a friend) to help you load, unload, and clean the unit. You will need a good flashlight, a couple of good locks, and some other things that any business would need. These all become business expenses that are valid to deduct from your taxes, if you find yourself doing well enough. It is important to treat this like a business, to make sure that you know how much you are spending, and how much you are making.

How much can you make?

Before we can start earning money, it's important to understand what the potential is, and what the process is for earning it. In order to make money buying storage units, you need to be able to buy items lower than you can expect to sell them, and then actually sell them. Seems easy, right? However, there is a fair amount of risk involved. You don't get to inspect the merchandise you are buying, and in some cases, you don't even get to see it at all. However, you can use this to your advantage, and still make a fair profit.

Just how much you can make by buying storage units depends on many factors. First, you need to decide how much you are able or willing to spend, and how much your costs are. When you are thinking about buying things for resale, you want to maximize how much of your capital is used to buy the goods, and minimize the overhead and other associated costs with the business. Additionally, you need to decide how much you are willing to invest. If you see a unit with a value of $20,000, and you can get it for $2,000, then you must have $2,000 to actually invest. The amount you participate is up to you, but it heavily influences how much money you can make.

Another factor is the merchandise you do wind up winning. There is a huge potential make money, no matter which items you wind up with, because there is such a wide range of items to be found. It's common to find things like furniture and bedding, as well as other household items. These large items are the first things that people move out of their homes when space becomes tight. You might also find other household items like toys, books, DVDs and clothing in the units.

The thing to keep in mind is to try to buy only the kinds of items that you can sell. You are looking for valuables, such as jewelry and collectables, or other items that have a ready market. Sadly, if a unit contains these things, they are probably sealed in boxes, or otherwise out of view. You may get lucky, and find that boxes are labeled, giving you a clue about what is inside.

Furniture is usually easy to resell, everyone needs furniture. It's also easy to see, as there is no way to hide a headboard to bed, or a dresser or changing table, inside of box. This kind of item, as well as regular kitchen items, appliances and baby items will sell consistently and easily, but rarely for the kind of profits that we are trying to achieve.

Sometimes, you can really strike gold, with items that are both small and very valuable. One strategy that people use for this is to try to buy lots of units with sealed boxes. You may walk away with clothing that will easily sell at a yard sale, or you may get lucky and find gold coins or baseball cards inside. But even if you don't come away with a diamond ring, you can still find things that sell easily, and for a quick profit.

Also, you need to do some research once you buy your unit. Never sell things immediately without knowing what you have. Anything that looks old, or valuable, or even antique should be researched so that you know what you are selling before you dispose of it. You don't want to sell something for a quick $10 profit when there was $1000 to be had.

Unless you are unlucky, and buy a unit that contains nothing but wadded up tissues and half used jars of spices, then you should always be on the lookout for how to make a profit from the items you buy. It's actually easier to make money than it is to lose it, as long as you buy correctly.

The Value of Research

If you are just getting started trying to profit from storage auctions, then it is important that you take the time to research all you can about the process. As easy as it seems, buy things low, sell them high, there are lots of things you can learn that will improve your profits and make things simpler along the way. The more you know, the more likely you are to turn a nice profit on your purchases.

One thing you need to research is the auction themselves. Learning how they work, what the process is, and how to get the best price will help you quite a bit. The best way to do this is to attend a few, with no intention of being a buyer. Learn how the registration process works, see how people are bidding, and get a feel for how much people are paying for certain kinds of units. You will also get to see what kind of merchandise are in these units, and you'll start to get a feel for how much you should expect to pay for what you see. You don't want to be bidding for the first time totally unprepared.

The easiest way to do this is to find an auction, and start asking questions. You generally don't want to do this at the auction itself, but rather you want to find one advertised, usually in the paper, but there are websites that track them as well. Give the auction company a call, and find out what their rules are. Do they only accept cash? It is a sealed bin auction, or do you get to inspect what you are buying? How many units are up for auction? All these questions will better prepare you for what you are about to embark on, and the more you know, the better off you will be. It will also give you an idea for which auctions you should be attending, and which ones you can skip, depending on the answers.

Now that you've researched the auction process, you should start looking up the items that you expect to be buying. Since you don't get to see what you are buying, or you only get a limited view, this can be a challenge. In some cases, you get to look inside, and peer around with a flashlight, but you still only get a minute or less to decide if you are going to buy it. You need to learn how to spot the items that will be profitable in resale. Even more, you need to learn to find items that are indicators of other items that may be in the unit. For instance, finding well-made, or antique furniture is a delight in itself. However, if you find these kinds of items along with a few sealed boxes, then that's a good sign that there may be something of quality within those boxes.

How do you research these kinds of things? Well, other than by buying guides like this one, your best bet is to attend some auctions and watch what happens.

Doing Research at the Auction Itself

If you've never been to an actual storage auction, then you should be sure to go to at least one, but probably a few, before you try to buy anything. If you try to buy a unit your first time out, you may find yourself quickly losing your investment, and getting frustrated in the process. You need to study how the auction process works, and the only way to do that is to attend. In this guide and others, we can explain how many auctions run, but each company has its own way of operating, and the rules can be different enough to make an impact.

There are generally two ways that storage unit auctions get announced. Either they are done on a regular schedule, like the first Friday of every month, or the storage facility will wait until they have enough units to auction off, and then announce it. Both methods work fine for the storage facility. However, on the regularly scheduled one, you are likely to get less units, since the driving factor behind them is the calendar, not the existence of units for sale.

Once you learn the schedule, and we'll talk about finding the auctions later in this guide, you should plan on attending at the right time, just to see how they run. Most auctions start right on time, and they happen right on the site of the storage facility, even if it is a third-party auctioneer doing the work. The auction company will open a unit, and allow for a few minutes to people to take a look inside, but not actually go inside of it. Some companies will let you touch boxes that you can reach from the door, but most will not. Remember, until the gavel falls on the auction, the items still legally belong to the renter of the unit – even if they are behind on their rent. In fact, they have right up to the very end to come and pay their tab, and the auction is cancelled.

But assuming the renter doesn't actually come in at the last second, you will only have a few minutes to decide what to do. There will be people around you who are ready to act – you need to be ready too, or get out of the way.

At most of these auctions, there will be regulars who come each and every time. These guys tend to know what they are doing, and they know how much money they can make from selling the goods inside. This means they have less risk in the unit than you do, and they can therefore bid more. One reason to go to a few auctions before you plan on bidding yourself is to start to recognize who these people are, and who you are potentially bidding against.

Once you do happen to win a unit, most auctions require the sale to be a cash-only sale. Some will take a cash deposit, and allow for the rest to be put on a credit card, but it's safer to assume that you are paying with cash on the spot. This means you need to have enough cash on hand to actually pay for your top bid, no running to the ATM or writing a IOU.

Most units go for under $500. So having that much on you will probably make you a contender for virtually any unit that comes up for sale. Some will go for more, and some will go for a lot more, but those are usually the ones that have a bunch of easily identifiable – and valuable – items that can be seen from the door.

If you win, the storage facility usually gives you 24 to 72 hours to clean out the unit entirely (called broom swept) and haul everything away. They aren't going to let you use their trash or their dumpsters, you bought it, you take care of it. You'll either need a small truck, or be prepared to take several trips. Also remember, this is your stuff now, and the lock has been cut off. You need to bring your own lock with you, to re-lock the unit and prevent anything from going missing. This can be a simple lock from the hardware store, and most padlocks are just fine. Many storage facilities will sell you one (not loan you one) but it's best not to count on this.

After you win, you can go through the unit immediately if you like, looking for small items of high value. You may even find that one of the other bidders is interested in buying an item off you right on the spot. This is only the first of many places you can resell the items you find within your unit.

At this point, you are going to need to pack up everything in the unit, whether you want it or not, and haul it away. Some of it you can bring right to the trash – again, not the trash at the facility. The rest of it you can bring to your own storage location, or even your own home garage. You may want to bring help with you to help load up, but if you do get 24-72 hours, you can also lock up the unit with your own lock, and come back with friends.

Later on, we'll talk about lots of different places and methods for selling what you wound up with.

What's that smell?

The first thing you need to do is figure out what you got. You might have really liked the looks of the unit from the outside, but you discovered that no one was bidding, not even the professionals we said to watch. It's possible that they know something that you don't. Maybe they didn't like the smell of the unit, or maybe they sensed some of the merchandise was damp or wet. Maybe they saw some things were broken that you couldn't see from the outside.

One thing you should be noticing is if the unit is climate controlled or not. Many facilities are outdoor facilities, and are just steel boxes on pavement. These are not often climate controlled, and can get hot in the summer, cold in the winter, and can leak. Heat and cold can do just as much damage as water, especially to collectible items, or things that can warp or bend. If you find yourself bidding on a unit that's outside, you should pay attention to every detail you can.

Depending on what you are interested in buying, you should pay attention to different details. Are the items in waterproof tubs, to keep the elements out? Is the furniture wrapped, or in tarps, or blankets? Or is the stuff just laying around the unit, in no real system or order? The condition of the unit itself is a real key to determining the condition of the merchandise. People will tend to take care of their good items, even in storage. Conversely, they won't take much care if they don't think the items were worth very much in the first place.

What you may hope to find, and what you may actually find

There are lots of things you can find in storage units. What you eventually take home with you will have a large impact on how much profit you can make from buying a unit. There is no easy answer. People use storage units for a variety of reasons, from their house being too small, to seasonal items, to protecting items that they want to keep but don't know what to do with. People also use them when they move, or when people pass away, or get married. There are probably as many reasons for having a storage unit as there are units themselves.

However, once you start going to auctions, you'll find a fair repetition in what you see in them.

What you can expect:

Appliances – You will often find appliances in storage units, both small and large. You'll find things as small as toasters and blenders, and all the way to washing machines and refrigerators.

These usually come from when two people that had homes decided to move in together. Appliances can be a great find, because they are easy to sell in yard sales or through Craigslist. If you find a unit full of these items, you are likely to pay more for the unit than for others. Again, the ease and speed of resale factors in to what people are willing to pay.

Home Decorations – These can come in many different flavors. This can be old paintings, or lamps, accent tables or other decorations. Many times, people redecorate or remodel their houses, but they don't want to throw out their old decorations. So, they wind up in storage. Usually, these pieces are in good condition, or else they would have just thrown them away, not stored them. These types of goods also will often sell in yard sales or on Craigslist. They are the kinds of things that everyone needs.

Holiday items – Go to enough auctions, and you will eventually come across an artificial Christmas tree, and a box of ornaments or wrapping paper. People will often over-decorate for the holidays, and then find that they don't have the room in their house to keep all the stuff. This is especially true if the auction is not between Halloween and New Years Day. Holiday items are tough. There's usually a good market for solid, artificial trees. They are expensive to buy, and lots of people have them. However, few people want to buy someone else's ornaments, or random decorations. When you see holiday items, only count the tree itself as valuable, unless you see things that you know are collectable, like Annalee dolls or Byers' Choice. Assume the rest is only of value to the original owner.

Kids' Stuff – Another common thing to find is children's things. This ranges from toys to books to cribs and changing tables. Kids outgrow stuff quickly, and more often than not, the stuff was still in usable shape when they outgrew it. The parents don't want to throw out something perfectly fine, so they store it until they can find someone who needs it. That someone can be you. Kids' stuff always sells, at yard sales, flea markets, and the lighter stuff such as clothing and DVDs sell easily on eBay and online. Finding a pile of good quality children's items is a real score.

Furniture – You will also certainly find furniture in units, and you'll find a lot of beds. The nice thing about it is that you can usually see it just fine from the outside. Normally, you can also get a feel for how old it is, and how sturdy it is. A solid wood dresser or bed frame can run in the hundreds of dollars, even more if it's an antique. Additionally, everyone needs furniture, so it's very easy to resell. On the downside, it's also usually heavy, so you'll need a truck and strong pair of arms or two to haul it away. But if you can handle it, good furniture is the easiest way to make a profit with a unit.

Tips for Bidding on Units

You only get a few minutes to examine a unit before you have to decide if you are going to be bidding on it or not. Because of that, and because you can't actually go in and examine what is inside the unit, you need to look for some signs for what may be inside.

For instance, if the items are strewn around the unit, in no order or organization, it's a sign that there is nothing good inside. There are two reasons why a unit would look like this. First, the person who rented the unit didn't take much care of their belongings, and therefore either didn't have things of much value, or didn't keep them in good shape. More likely, though, is second, the renter of the unit came back to take all the good stuff out, and then defaulted on the rent. Since they knew they weren't coming back, they didn't much mind what state they left the unit in.

On the other end of the spectrum are sealed boxes. Boxes of many different sizes and shapes can often be a sign that they contain household items. People who are moving, or putting their own belongings away, tend to use whatever boxes happen to be on hand at the time. However, boxes that are all the same size and shape could be commercial goods, or from a store closing. Even better, if they are stacked neatly or even pallet stacked, that means that someone was paying attention when they stored them, again indicating that they may be of some value.

You also want to examine the condition of the unit itself. If it looks like it's been undisturbed for years, say by seeing lots of dust, or other signs of non-use, then it may be good for certain kinds of items, and bad for others. Time and age can be fine for furniture and collectibles, much worse for appliances and clothing. Units that are climate controlled suffer from this less, of course, but even still, do you want a toaster from 20 years ago?

Choose wisely

Choosing the right auction to participate in can have a big impact on how much profit you make. Before you spend time going to an auction, try to find out what it is they are auctioning off. See if it's a sealed bin auction where you don't even get to look inside, or if it's one where you get to examine the goods without going in. Sometimes, auctions are for sealed cartons or boxes, not entire units. Knowing what kind of auction you are attending will help out from the start.

If you are at an auction where you can see the merchandise, then it's important to try to take a look at what brands things are. This takes some practice. But an upright vacuum from Sears can cost $50, while the same vacuum from Dyson is $400, and if it's an Oreck, can be nearly $1000. It's worth it to learn the key brands of items, so that you can recognize them when you see them.

But viewing name brands isn't just important because of their value for resale. Seeing name brands is another indicator of the quality of the merchandise that you cannot see. Someone who is willing to shell out $1000 for a vacuum probably also has other high-end merchandise in storage, and probably other name brands as well. These kind of goods are the kinds that hold their value, and create profits on resale.

One thing to watch for is items that may have significant value to the owner, but not to anyone else. People tend to save mementos and keepsakes that mean a lot to them, but wouldn't sell to anyone else for any kind of profit. However, there are certain kinds of keepsakes that will sell, things like jewels, of course, but also things like wedding dresses and other bridal things. There is a huge market for both "gently used" bridal items, as well as "vintage" gowns and accessories. And again, if you see items like these, it's a sign that they are saving their valuables, and that there may be other such things to be found within.

A unit filled with boxes is a particular challenge, and one that requires other cues to determine if they may hold anything valuable. Do the boxes have moving labels on them? If so, that means someone paid to have the contents moved, indicating some value inside. Are they still sealed with original tape? If so, it might represent either items that aren't needed that often, or it might be the case where a two people moved in together, causing a duplication of items. If they look like they have been opened and resealed often, that can be a sign that they contain items that get used quite a bit – and the boxes may now be missing key items. Practice and experience will tell you the things to look for in these kinds of items.

The key here is to use your judgment. Figure out what kind of auction you are attending before you decide to attend. Use cues to try to take a guess at what could be lurking inside of a unit. And stay away from items and units that look like they might not have valuables, or that the good stuff might have been taken out already.

Common Mistakes

Remember, money is made at these auctions by buying items that you can later resell for a profit. We will talk later in this guide about strategies for reselling, but as with most other investments, you make the money when you buy, not when you sell. Having the proper strategy for buying units is much more important than your strategy for selling the goods you wind up winning.

Here are a few common mistakes you should look to avoid:

Getting to an auction late: In some auctions, if you arrive late, you are prevented from bidding at all. This is actually for a good reason – if you arrived late, then you didn't hear all the rules, and you haven't agreed to them. But, arriving just on time isn't good, either. If you are planning to participate in an auction, you should try to arrive 10-20 minutes early, so that you can see who else arrives, and maybe get a feel for what people are looking to get. You'll find people looking for furniture, collectibles, or flea market stuff. Depending on what you are trying to obtain, this can be useful information. You should also be looking for familiar faces, so that you know who to watch out for when you are bidding.

Going too far out of your way: One of the hidden costs of buying a storage unit is that you need to haul everything away. If you are attending an auction too far away, then you are probably limited to buying a unit that will fit in whatever vehicle you happened to bring. This means that if a great unit comes up at a great price, but your truck isn't big enough, you have to pass on it. Better to either stay closer to home, where you can make two or three trips if necessary.

Not knowing the rules: If you do find yourself travelling, or spending a lot of time on an auction, you want to make sure you are clear on the rules. Is it a cash-only sale? How long will you have to empty out the unit? Are the units sealed? Can you go in them? Are they cartons-only? You should make sure you know what you are going into, before you even consider buying anything.

Not having patience: Buying storage units has an element of skill along with a large element of luck. You may make a killing on your first unit, but I wouldn't count on it. The goal is to buy many units that all have the possibility of turning out profitable. Some of them will, some won't, but on average, you'll come out ahead. The more you buy, the better your odds are of finding something interesting. But if you go to a few auctions, and win nothing, or if your first few are non-profitable, don't give up. Know that it takes time and experience to do well in the business.

Not knowing what you are looking to get: Are you looking for furniture? Collectables? Kids' clothing? Whatever it is that you are trying to win doesn't matter, what matters is that you know what you are trying to win. If you don't know what you are looking to take home, then you will be unfocused, and not sure what it is you are doing. Whatever it is you are trying to get, knowing what it is ahead of time will go a long way towards getting it right.

Not bringing the right tools: You should know to bring a flashlight, so that you can poke into dark corners of units that you are allowed to look into. Without a strong flashlight, this is very difficult. You should be bringing at least one lock, to lock up your unit should you win one. If you don't, you are probably forced to buy one from the storage company, which will probably not come at a great price. You should also be bringing a vehicle able to haul off at least things of medium size. Without it, you'll need to come back, costing you time, effort and gas, while you are trying to make a profit on the unit. Without the right tools at your disposal, you will have a difficult time doing well.

What not to do

While not necessarily a list of common mistakes, here is a collection of things you want to be sure you don't do as part of your storage auction business.

Don't be unprepared. Call ahead, and find out the rules, and have enough cash on hand to cover your purchases if it is a cash only sale. Ask what information you'll need to have to register as a buyer, and make sure you are there on time.

Don't fall in love with a unit. After attending several auctions, you may find that you haven't won anything yet, or that you haven't found anything you like yet. Then when you do finally find something you like, you overpay for it. Don't do this. Remember to have patience, and we make our money when we buy.

Don't throw out your items. Even if you buy a unit full of worthless junk, there are lots of good ways to get rid of it. Sell things in huge lots, have a yard sale, or even donate to charity or goodwill. As long as the things are useable, they don't even have to be very nice. But someone's loss is someone else's gain.

Don't pay to throw out your items, either. Even if you do find yourself in a position to throw away your items, it will drastically hurt your profits if you have to pay someone to haul things away. You've turned an expense into a double expense. Always be on the lookout for places that will take decent quality merchandise off your hands for free. There are lots of them out there.

Don't only have one method of selling. There are many different ways to resell your items that we will cover in a few pages. But note that there is no one single way to do it. Depending on your situation, the item, and lots of different factors, you may find you need to have several different methods to sell your stuff.

Finally, don't give up! You will probably not make money on your first unit, unless you are lucky.

Watch the professionals you see at the auctions, and you'll find that they are buying more than one unit every time, and they buy something every week. This is because while many units break even, not all units turn a profit. You need to keep at it, and keep plugging.

Chapter Two: Running the Business

Make no mistake, if you are going to get into the Storage Auction business, then you do need to run it like a business. You need to have the system and processes created so that you can focus on making money and turning a profit, while minimizing your costs and time. In order to do this properly, you need to understand everything that goes into the business, from finding the auctions to selling the items you purchase. The better you understand how everything works, the better you will get at doing all the tasks efficiently, saving you time and money.

There are four main steps to running this business:

1. Locating the auctions
2. Determining what kinds of items you would like to acquire
3. Transporting and processing units that you win
4. Reselling the items that you do win

Each of these steps is vital to the business, and you can save yourself lots of time – and increase your profits, if you can do them quickly and accurately, every time.

Locating Auctions

Finding auctions is actually pretty easy. It's to everyone's advantage to make sure that the most people show up for the auctions as possible. The auction company and the storage unit company only make money if people come to the auctions and bid, so they have no reason to keep the information private. But, you won't see them advertising on television commercials, because advertising has costs which they can't recoup all that easily. They have two goals, sell the most money, and sell quickly. But most of all, make sure that every unit sells. It's not worth it to them to pay an extra $1000 if they are only going to make an additional $50.

That being said, there are two different sources of information for storage auctions, the auction companies and the storage facilities. Finding the storage facilities are easy, they are all listed in the yellow pages. Most of these companies are incredible low-tech, and even if they have a website, they are unlikely to have kept it up to date. Therefore, your best bet is to call them, and find out what their auction calendar looks like. Sometimes, they have regular auctions, either once a month or once a quarter. Other companies will only hold an auction when they have enough units to auction off. You won't know which is which until you call and ask.

Finding the auctions companies is a little bit different. For all the storage unit companies in your area, there are probably only a handful of auction houses. You can google "Storage Auctions" and probably find one or two companies in your area that handles them. If that doesn't give you any information, you can try http://www.auctionzip.com/, which is a website that has a listing of all live auctions going on your area, storage auctions and otherwise.

Once you understand where the auctions are in your area, you want to start figuring out which ones you will attend, and then attend a few. You want to keep two things in mind, minimizing your time, and minimizing your expenses. Both of these are what will eventually cost your business money if you don't actively manage them. You want to participate in as many auctions as you can, but you don't want to drive three hours each way, just to attend one auction. Making sure you are using your time efficiently is key to turning a profit.

Finally, an as we covered before, once you know what auctions you will be attending, you want to go to a few of them ahead of time. You want to make sure you understand the rules and the cadence of the auction, as well as get to know the regular attendees and about what to expect. This kind of knowledge will be immensely valuable when the times comes to actually bid on items.

Creating Your Own Auction Calendar

You have two needs when it comes to deciding which auctions you will attend. You want to make sure that you are attending as many auctions as fit your schedule, whether that means one auction a week, or several per day. You also want to make sure that you are using your time and available resources properly by making a plan for which auctions you will attend, and when. With this calendar in hand, you can have a plan for when you expect to be working at your new business, and about when you can hope to have new items to come in.

Additionally, you may have people helping you out with this business. It can be someone with a truck, who is helping you haul stuff away, or it can be someone who knows about furniture, or can help identify items that you find. Maybe it's another investor, someone who has money at stake in how you do. Whatever the reason, it's another reason to have a calendar of auctions that you are attending, so that your support team knows what is going on. Without them knowing when and where they are supposed to be, you won't be nearly as effective in acquiring new items.

Figuring out how much stuff is worth

Before you attend an auction, and certainly before you actually win anything, you should know what types of items you are interested in winning. Are you interested in getting regular household items, like furniture, appliances or general housewares? How about electronics, stereo equipment or computers? Or are you looking for children's items, clothing, or toys? Are you mostly interested in collectables? If you don't know what it is that you are looking for, then you'll have a hard time deciding how much items and units are worth when you see them.

One way to get an idea for what things will sell for is to visit the types of places you plan on selling your items ahead of time. If you plan on using flea markets, yard sales, or craigslist to sell, say, furniture, you should spend some time going to these places, and getting a feel for what sells, and how much things sell for. You can sometimes get this information by asking the vendors, but they tend to be reluctant to tell you the truth. A better way to find out is to simply watch what people are buying, and see how much they pay for it. Having this knowledge will go a long way to determining how much you should pay for a storage unit.

If you plan on selling on eBay, you have a much easier time of it, as eBay keeps a history of all the items that have sold, and what they have sold for. Many items are not recommended to sell on ebay, but an awful lot of the items that you find at auction would be just fine to sell. Searching eBay's history will tell you how often things have sold, and how much sellers have gotten in return.

There are many ways to research the resale value of commonly found items, but one of the more important factors is having this information with you at the auction itself. Since you are only given a few minutes to decide if you are going to bid, and how much you are willing to pay, having this information with you will be a great asset. This can mean having all your information in a notebook, on index cards, or on your smartphone. Whatever you need to do to have more information than the rest of the bidders will put you at a distinct advantage over them.

Deciding what to keep and what to throw away

No matter how good you are at identifying units and items to buy, not everything you find is going to be worth keeping. This can be true even in a unit that holds fantastic stuff, you'll find that there are items that you simply do not want, or cannot sell. Since most storage auctions come with a very tight time frame for when you need to empty them out, you are faced with some very quick decisions. What do you keep, and what do you get rid of. This snap decision can have a large impact on how profitable you are, since deciding to keep something not only means that you need to haul it to your own location, but also that you need to store it, inventory it, and do all the things that you would do for items of high resale value. Sometimes, simply throwing things out, or donating them, will save you time and effort – and therefore money – in the long run.

So, when you do win a storage unit, you need to quickly separate the items you are going to keep from the items you are going to throw away. Some of it is obvious; anything broken, damaged or stained is unlikely to make you any money, so there's no sense in processing them at all. But some of it takes an eye to know what will resell. If you have an item in reasonable shape, but no one is going to buy it, then there is no sense in going through the effort to keep it either. Once you have your stuff separated between the things you want to keep, and the things you want to throw away, pack up the good stuff with some care, and take it away to process.

Dealing With Trash

Make no mistake; there is an awful lot of junk in storage units. Even units that contain a large quantity of saleable goods can still contain a bunch of trash that you need to find an easy and cheap way to throw away. Ideally, it won't be the entire unit, but even that is a possibility.

What do we mean by trash? It could mean many things depending on who you ask, but for the purposes of this discussion, we mean things that you cannot, or should not, sell for a profit. This isn't a judgment on other people's things, it's simply a matter of business. We are trying to make a profit by buying this unit, anything that we can't resell is trash, simple as that.

For instance, if you find files full of personal information, financial records, old pictures or high school yearbooks, we can call this stuff trash. We can't resell any of this for a profit, and worse, we are obligated to turn over most of this back to the storage company. Virtually all storage companies have a policy about this kind of item, as soon as you discover them in the unit, you need to return it, and they hold on to it for a certain period while they try to return it to the rightful owner.

Another example is well worn clothing. This may be stained or not, or may just be clothing that has clearly been worn repeatedly. It may be torn, need mending, or need a solid fumigating. Whatever the reason, it's not something that you can resell.

Depending on what you find, it's possible that you can find a way to monetize it. For instance, old clothing can be cut apart into scraps, or the buttons saved, or even mended. Pictures that are very,

very old may have some value to collectors of nostalgia. This can take a lot of work, and may not be worth your effort, depending on how much you win.

One thing to consider is a charitable donation. Just because something isn't saleable for a profit doesn't mean that it's totally valueless. Lots of things have a good amount of use left in them, but no one is really willing to pay for them. Consider a fully working, but somewhat old toaster. You might get $5 for it in tag sale, but that's hardly worth the effort. How about a nice winter coat that's missing a button? Maybe an ironing board? There are lots of examples of things that a charity would happily take in that you would have no real possibility of turning a profit with. Before throwing something away, consider giving it to a charity.

Another thing to explore is throwing the things you don't want out right there at the facility. Most facilities don't allow this, but some do, and some will let you do it for a small fee. This may very well be worth it. Since you are right there, you save all the transportation costs, labor costs, time and effort, if you can throw things out while you are there. Even for a fee, this may be the right thing to do, and it can never hurt to ask – or even often to pay for the service.

If that doesn't work, your next stop is the junkyard or the dump, or whatever your local town calls it. If you have an item that is broken, you can't sell, and you don't even feel good about giving away, then you should really throw it out. Some dumps charge a fee by the item, some charge an annual fee or charge you a fee to get a sticker. Call around your town and towns around you, and find out what the best price is in your area. If you are going to be buying several storage units, I can promise you that you will be throwing a lot of things away. Having a good source for trash will be a helpful asset to you.

Of course, you may be able to give your items away. You can put your items on the sidewalk with a sign that says "Free." Craigslist has a section specifically for free items. If you are having a yard sale, you can have a section just full of items for free. Lots of people like free stuff, and aren't all that picky if it needs a little bit of repair. Be careful not to expend too much of your own time and energy, though. Don't deliver free stuff, and don't offer to repair it yourself. You may be willing to help load it into someone's truck, but that's about as far as you should go. You are giving something away, don't also give away your time and money to do it!

There are a lot of ways to get rid of stuff you don't want, or can't resell. It's important to track how much disposing of these things will cost you, of course. Ideally, you'll have many ways to get rid of stuff for free or nearly free. Paying to get rid of items you are going to lose money on is a double loser, and should be avoided if at all possible.

Keeping a Selling Calendar

Earlier, we talked about the importance of keeping a calendar of buying opportunities. Knowing when the auctions are, and creating a schedule so that you can maximize the number of auctions you can attend is a good thing. But it's equally important to keep a calendar of when you plan on selling your items.

If you are selling things live, then you have a lot of things to coordinate. If you are selling at a yard sale, you need to know when to have enough people on hand to tend it and run it. If you are going to a flea market, you'll need transportation, as well as figuring out how to handle the kind of traffic that a flea market generates.

You may do group yard sales, which need to be managed separately, or maybe you want to do more than one in the same day, each with a different area of focus. Managing this is important, and is a challenge. Keeping a good calendar of selling events can be as important as keeping a good calendar of buying events.

If you are selling online, you need to keep track of start and end times, as well as the inventory you have on hand. You don't want to be selling something in a flea market that you are currently selling online. Selling online also comes with other trappings, such as taking pictures, posting them for people to view, and scheduling start and ending times. If you are selling online, you should plan to have something selling all the time, but not so much that you get overwhelmed with the amount of work it takes to do it properly. Failure to properly deliver is worse than not selling your items at all.

Having enough cash

Like most businesses, one of the most important things is making sure you are well capitalized. In the case of the storage auction business, this means having enough cash. When you win an auction, you will probably be asked to pay for it immediately and probably in cash. Since most units go for under $1000, this isn't a hardship for most buyers, but it does mean that if a very good unit comes up for sale, the more cash you have in your pocket represents the more that you can buy.

This is another case where knowing what you want to buy will be a helpful guide in deciding how much cash you need to have with you. Furniture tends to have a higher resale value, and therefore, a higher purchase price. General housewares tend to have a lower purchase price. Knowing what kinds of items you are looking to buy will be a factor in determining how much cash you'll need to bring with you.

But it's not the only factor you need to consider. After the auction is over, you may want to pay some of the other participants to help you load your truck. Or you may find a storage facility that is willing to let you throw out the unwanted items onsite – as long as you pay for the privilege. You may also find yourself interested in buying items from a buyer who won a unit that you wanted – or you only wanted a small piece of. Cash is the universal currency in this business, and making sure you have enough of it will be a key to your success.

As a seller, you may find yourself running a garage sale, or working a flea market. Most of your customers will expect you to be able to make change for virtually any amount, at any time of the day. In fact, not being able to give proper change may cause you to lose a sale, and selling the items is what this business is all about. Remember to keep your personal cash and your business cash separate. It may seem silly to "make change for yourself" but it is important to keep your business and personal expenses separate. This is important not only for tax purposes, but also so that you know how much money you are making overall.

Have Transportation

This seems obvious, but it is often underestimated. You are going to be buying a lot of stuff. Even a small storage unit is 80 square feet, which is much, much more than you can hope to fit into a Ford Explorer. You need to have access to a pickup truck, van, or trailer, to haul your winnings. One of the most depressing sight is someone who wants to bid and win a unit, but then realizes that the vehicle that they brought isn't going to be big enough to carry it all away. Don't allow lack of proper transportation to be a reason for you not to win your unit. You don't need to have this transportation permanently, you can borrow or rent it if you need to do so, but you must have some kind of reliable access to a vehicle big enough to cart way whatever you win.

Of course, you are going to need to put gas in the truck, and insure it, and you get to deduct general depreciation on it. If it's your personal truck, then there are guidelines to use to figure out how much of the expenses you can deduct. The important thing is to keep track of what the vehicle is costing you, not just for tax purposes, but also that you can keep a handle on your expenses.

Having a vehicle is important, but you'll need more than just that. You are probably going to need all the equipment that moving companies use. This means blankets to protect the items, dollies or handtrucks for help in hauling, and straps or ropes to keep things in place. If you have a pickup or other open-air truck, then you might want to buy tarps, to make sure that everything stays protected from weather.

Finally, you'll need some other things that most movers know all about. A good pair of canvas gloves will be invaluable if you are digging through boxes, furniture, and broken items. Strapping tape, garbage bags, and moving boxes or crates will also be of assistance. There is no guarantee that the items you buy will be in boxes or anything set up for easy moving.

Having people to help

Of course, all the equipment in the world won't be as valuable as having an extra pair of hands to help you out. There are a couple of strategies for getting people to help you out.

First, getting family or friends to help you out is usually pretty easy. Auctions are fun and exciting and different, and you'll often find that people you know simply want to be a part of it. You might find that you don't even really need to pay them for their trouble, beyond a cup of coffee and maybe a good lunch afterwards. Some of your friends may even want to know what the whole thing is all about, and will want to come along with someone who knows what is going on, just to learn it. Be prepared to be patient, and to explain a lot of things to your helpers. But remember that having someone else help you load items into your truck is worth an awful lot.

Another idea is to add them as part of the business. Your friends or family may be interested enough in buying items for themselves, or for resale on their own. Or, they may be willing to split the take 50/50, or some other split that you agree with. This can be rewarding, but it can also be dangerous. Winning an auction is a fairly solitary thing, you have a price in your mind, and you aren't willing to go over it. But if there are two of you bidding on a single unit, you certainly don't want to be bidding against each other, and you don't want to be driving the price up based on your conflicting interests. Having a partner is incredibly helpful, but not if it gets in the way of making a profit.

Finally, you can also just hire people. You can still hire your friends or family if you like, or you can find people on Craiglist or through a temp agency. If you do this, you need to decide how you are going to pay, if it's going to be by the hour, or a flat fee for a day. Or maybe you'll pay more if you win something that needs to be hauled away. You should stay away from paying people a percentage of the profit, as the record keeping that it requires is almost never worth it.

Of course, if you do hire and pay people to help you out, you should keep track of it. As usual, you need this information not only for tax purposes, but also so that you have a firm grasp on the inflows and outflows of your business. If you buy a unit for $100 and resell it for $400, that's fantastic – unless it cost you $500 to haul and process the items. Knowing what you are spending on is vital to your success.

Having a place to put all the items

Similar to having a good enough truck, having a place to store your stuff may be something you already have on hand. It could be your garage or basement, or maybe under a tarp in your backyard. If you have a big enough house, you can use a spare bedroom, or even a spare closet, to keep many of the items you'll wind up acquiring.

If you find that you have items that need to be kept in climate controlled location, inside your house may be the only good option. But for things that won't get damaged outside, then keeping in the garage – or investing in weatherproof storage bins, isn't a bad idea. One of the downsides of keeping the items in your house in increasing the clutter you have to deal with in your everyday life. Some people find the cost savings more than makes up for it.

If you are able to do so, then keeping things where you can work on them is a plus. If you plan on selling via a garage sale or flea market, having the ability to lay everything out for organization, cleaning and pricing will greatly help your efforts.

Even better if you can actually set up your garage sale "store" the night before, and have everything ready when the buyers show up.

And of course, you want, you can get your own storage unit. These have the benefit of being outside of your house, and usually being climate controlled. They will also help you keep your expenses separate for when it comes time to report how your business is doing. The downside is that this is an extra expense. You don't want to become exactly the kind of person that you are buying units from in the first place!

Chapter Three: Reselling

Even small storage units can be over 100 cubic feet of space. When you win your first one, you are going to find yourself with lots of things to dig through, and to find a place to resell. You have two different goals – make your money back as soon as possible, and make as much money as you can. Sometimes, these are different things. Because of this, you need to have a strategy for how you are going to be reselling the items that you get.

You'll need to know how much things will resell for, where the best place to see them are, and how to balance between selling them quickly, and selling them for the most. Within any single unit will be items appropriate for a pawn shop, yard sale, eBay or Craigslist. In fact, you will be likely to find all four kids of items in the same unit.

It's up to you to decide what your strategy is going to be. You may decide to take your more valuable items and put them on eBay, or a live auction house. You may schedule a yard sale, or go to a big flea market. Each type of selling strategy has its own cost, both in actual money you have to spend in fees, and in how much effort it will take for you to make a sale.

Tips for Reselling

When deciding how you are going to resell the items that you get, there are three factors to consider.

They are:

- Expenses – how much is it going to cost you to make the sale? This should include direct fees, like flea market entrance fees, or the cost of gas if you are delivering an item, or just your time, if you are going to be spending all day doing it.
- Likelihood of selling – How likely is it that you are actually going to make a sale? It's a real hassle to drag all your items to a flea market, and then have to bring them all back.
- Final selling price – Where will you wind up with the highest prices for your items? This has a different answer for each kind of item, but must be factored into the decision.

Keeping your expenses low is important. Ebay can be fast and easy, but they take 6% or more of the price. Craigslist is free, but unless you have an item perfect for it, you might not get a buyer, and even then, not for the highest price. If you live some place that has a lot of drive-by traffic, then a yard sale makes a lot of sense. But if you have a lot of expensive valuables or jewelry, these aren't the kinds of items that people attending yard sales are looking to buy. Figuring out where and how to sell is just as important as figuring out where and what to buy.

Before you sell

Before we get into actual selling strategies, there are a few things you should do with the items first. If you have clothing, or things with small pockets or enclosures, you want to open everything up. People tend to hide their things in their pockets or in drawers – or they may have forgotten that they left $100 or more in the pockets of their pants. It's possible to make back the entire cost of a unit simply by finding stuff left there by accident.

Next, look for anything that looks like an antique. This includes things you wouldn't expect, like a vase, a mirror, or a figurine. If you think you have such an item, you can try to research the item online. In a few minutes and a little work with search engines, you can usually get an idea if what you have is possibly something that's very valuable. If you do find that it's a possibility, it's usually best to get something appraised by an expert. A good tip for this is to tell them that you are getting it appraised for insurance purposes. If you tell them that you have no clue what it is or what it's worth, an unscrupulous appraiser may give you a low figure, and then attempt to buy the item from you on the spot. Unless you want the money in had for a lower figure, simply take the information that the appraiser gives you.

Finally, take each item and spread it out in the light. Look for stains, rips, or anything that you think you can mend or clean. You will generally get much more for an item that is in clean and good-looking condition, than one that is dirty, ripped or broken.

Selling immediately

Sometimes, you have the chance to sell your items immediately. By immediately, we're talking about right there at the storage auction, to one of the other auction bidders. Right there at the auction are going to be dozens of folks, with cash on hand, who are disappointed that they are leaving with nothing. Not only might they be interested in buying for their business the same as you are, but they may also be interested in buying for themselves.

Once you buy a unit, you are allowed to go inside and start working with the goods. You do not have to wait until the auction is over. Remember, usually you are given 48-72 hours to make the unit "broom swept" clean, but that doesn't mean you should wait. The first 30 minutes after the auction is the first chance you have to resell the items. This is especially good if people are wandering around the facility, looking at other units. If you wait even an hour, you may miss the opportunity to resell the items, and quickly recoup your investment.

Imagine you open your unit, and you find a nice set of golf clubs, maybe a Calloway driver or some Ping irons. Even used, these can be worth hundreds of dollars. You want to take these out and set them up where people can see them. You can also put them in your truck, or some other place where people will be able to inspect what you got. Remember, the people around you not only have money and are motivated to buy something; they are also going to be curious about the deal that they passed up. You can also yell, or sound a little excited if you find something you think you can easily resell. People will be even more curious, and come over to check why you are so excited.

There are lots of reasons why you would want to try to sell right away. In fact, it may be the case that you are willing to accept a little bit less of a selling price right at the facility. Selling right then saves you the time and effort to load your truck with the item, drive it away, process it, store it, and then figure out how to sell it. It allows you to focus on the other items in the unit, giving you more time and space to properly break down and take away everything you just bought. It may even save you an entire trip, which would save you significant time and money. Finally, if you are lucky, often you can sell one or two items for most or all of the original cost of the unit, allowing you to "play with house money" for the rest of the items. Walking away from the auction with a truckload of items for free is always a good feeling.

Flea Markets

Selling at flea markets is an easy way to get the cash out of your items. To do it efficiently takes a bit of coordination, however. Flea markets are generally on weekends, and usually in open air fields, or in large warehouses. Storage auctions are usually on weekdays. So, if you don't have a good calendar of events, you may be stuck buying items, loading your truck, unloading the truck, reloading it for the flea market, then unloading it again. Proper coordination will save you lots of time and effort.

Many flea markets require that you have a reseller license. This is actually okay; there are other advantages to getting one. For instance, if you do not have a reseller id, then the storage auction may charge you sales tax on the final value of the unit that you win. With a reseller id, you don't have to pay this, which can save you 5-10%, depending on where you live. It also helps make your taxes look cleaner, as you have an actual business to operate under. Finally, having a license may open up other opportunities for you in other venues. If you do not have one yet, you can usually either contact your local town hall or the organizers of the flea market themselves. Either place is interested in getting you a license, so they are motivated to helping you out.

When you show up for the flea market, focus on getting your area set up immediately. If you have a table, or a tent, or folding chairs, or some other display, the earlier you can get things started the better. Flea markets have three main kinds of customers. There are people who come right as the gates open, looking for the best stuff. There are people who come right as it is ending, looking for a great deal on items that you don't really want to have to take back home with you. And in the middle, there are lots and lots of people who are just browsing. Being set up quickly helps you get the attention of the first kind of person – the person looking for good stuff, and not the second two kinds, who are just looking for deals.

There are lots of strategies for flea markets. You can put a sticker on each item, and price each item differently. Or you can put things on tables or display units, with a "Everything for $1" sign. Or you can use a color-coding system. Whatever you use, pricing can be done many ways.

The weakness to flea markets is the price at which you can expect to sell your items. Even the people looking for quality merchandise are still looking to get it at a rock bottom price. If you have rare items, or collectables, it takes a certain type of buyer to show up to buy your item. However, if you have everyday household items, small appliances, clothing, or baby items, then you can easily walk away with $100-$500 at the end of the day.

Experiment with a different mix of products, and different flea markets, and eventually you will find the right formula to maximize how much money you are bringing in.

Selling at Yard Sales

If you have a lot of little items, furniture or a lot of household items in your inventory, setting up a yard sale may be a good choice. There are lots of advantages to having a one. For one, you don't need a reseller id. You also get to decide the date and time that your yard sale will occur. Plus, you don't usually have to put all your items in your truck and haul them away, you can set up your yard sale at your own leisure, and only sell when you are ready. It's a good way to start out.

It's also a good way to operate if you are really doing this as a side business. It allows you to maintain control over the amount of work that the business requires, and when that work happens. It gives you the time to set your store up, and gives you some experience about what people are looking to buy, and how much they are willing to pay. And best of all, for the most part, yard sales are free, or really cheap to hold, if you need to buy a few posters.

The problem with yard sales is similar to those with flea markets. You won't be getting the highest selling price for your items, as people who frequent yard sales are also generally seeking deals. You also are limited to the number of people you can attract, so if you don't live in an area with a lot of people, or a lot of drive-by traffic, you may have a hard time getting people interested and involved in your sale.

Even still, it's a great way to clear some inventory, and make a little extra cash in the process.

Selling to a pawn shop

If you live in an area where there are good pawn shops, then this is a great place to get cash for certain kinds of items. They are mostly good for items that have a high intrinsic value, like silver, gold, watches and jewelry. If you are just looking to get quick cash for these items, then a pawn shop is probably the way to go. They'll give you money on the spot, and almost certainly buy any item of value.

Of course, pawn shops are also in the business to make money, so while they will tell you the truth about how much your item is worth, you can expect to get less than that. If they don't do that, eventually the pawn shop goes out of business. But it is usually helpful to get cash out of your items in a hurry, or at the very least, know how much cash you can get out of them in a hurry.

If there is a pawn shop near you, you should try to build a relationship with the owner. Not only is it a good place to get money for the items that you buy, it can also be a source of items to resell elsewhere. Once you have a good feel for the resell market, having a source of goods is always a helpful thing.

Selling your items on eBay

If you don't mind doing a little extra paperwork, then selling on eBay can be the best venue for you to sell some of your items. Selling on eBay has a lot of advantages. You can sell a few items each day, and have them end on days that are convenient to you. If you properly describe your item, and take good pictures, then you will usually get a fair price at the end. In fact, since you are exposing your item to many more potential buyers, you will usually get a higher price than you would get at a yard sale or flea market.

One drawback to eBay is the fees that you have to pay. At a flea market, you generally pay by the amount of space you are taking up, and it doesn't matter how many items you have. On eBay, you pay a per-item charge. So, if you have a lot of items that are worth $1 or so, then eBay can be an expensive proposition. But if you have items of reasonable value ($20 or more) then eBay is often your best bet to get the best price.

There are lots of other books that can help you get the most out of an eBay auction, so we won't go into the details much right now. However, particularly with storage unit items, pictures and descriptions are important. Since virtually all the items that you are reselling are used, people want to understand the condition, and the best way to explain that is through pictures.

The last consideration for eBay is the cost of shipping. Since more than 99% of the sales on eBay require you to ship the item to the buyer, if you have a difficult item to ship, then you may have costs, time or annoyance figuring out how to get the item to the buyer. While eBay does allow you to charge the buyer for shipping, it's generally not acceptable to charge for the time it will take for you to properly pack the item for transit, or for the materials you will need to buy to ship it. This means items that are big, weight over 20 pounds, or are unusually sized can be hassle to sell online.

Selling on eBay has its plusses. When you have an item that is easily shippable, in good condition, and can be photographed easily, you will be able to get as close to fair value on eBay than anywhere else. It comes with some fees and some work, but it is usually worth it.

Selling on Craigslist

The best features of yard sales include low costs, not having to deliver the items, cash transactions, and quick sales. There is a venue that gives you most of these benefits, but also gives you the benefits of being online, and gaining the traffic from a highly used website. I am referring, of course, to Craigslist.org.

Craigslist is similar to an online yard sale, where people post what they have for sale, a few pictures, and the price. Usually, the buyer will come to your location, look at the item, and decide for themselves if they want to buy it. Very similar to how a yard sale works, except your yard sale is limited to the people in your neighborhood, while Craigslist is limited to the people who are willing to drive to your location, which can be 10 or more times as many people.

Craigslist also has the ability for people to search on specific keywords, or browse specific categories. Say you buy a storage unit full of baby clothing and electronics. These are likely to be two separate types of customers, requiring two different Craigslist postings. If you have a single yard sale, you'll get a mish-mash of people, and not really have a focused ability to get the highest price for your items.

Craigslist also gives you the ability to group items together. If you bought a huge box of CDs, they may be difficult to sell individually, but much easier to sell as a lot, such as 10 for $10. The same is true for golf clubs, clothing, or baby items. Selling things as a lot has an advantage to both buyer and seller. The buyer gets good value for their purchase, and the seller is able to clear out space and inventory, to make room for more items.

Craigslist has its own issues, such as spammers and scammers, but these are easily controlled. Always demand cash for your purchases, and never ship to a Craigslist buyer, always meet in person. If you don't want to meet with the person at your home, choose a nearby public place, like the parking lot of a supermarket, or some other place where people are always around. Many of the problems with Craigslist are easily overcome.

Selling online

There are many benefits to selling online, be it eBay or Craigslist. You get to set your own schedule and control your own time. You also will reach a lot more people than you would by selling at a yard sale or at a pawn shop. In general, you'll get the highest selling price for these items, simply because there are so many people shopping online.

It does come with some things to watch for, though. The auction site eBay has fees that can take a small bite out of your items, and has some challenges when it comes to shipping items. Craigslist is free, but may come with a little bit of spam or scammers.

A little experience in the area will go a long way in understanding how to make the most of your online selling activities.

Conclusion: Are Storage Auctions Right for you?

Many people are making money buying items in storage auctions and reselling them. But you need to decide if the business is right for you. The opportunity for making money has never been greater. Due to the economy, people are abandoning or forgetting about the items they have put in storage, allowing you to buy good quality items at a very low price. You may be able to go to several auctions a week, and view lots of items.

There is some risk, however. You don't generally get to see what it is that you are bidding on; it's usually a blind item. While you may come away with gold coins or expensive furniture, you may also come away with stained clothing or useless paperwork.

Despite this risk, people do make a significant profit every time they buy a unit. Sometimes it is as low as $200, sometimes it is in the thousands or more. A lot of the profit comes from luck, skill, and experience. Buying more units will lead to a higher output, simply because you have more chances to find something great inside your unit.

Knowing what you are looking for can be a big benefit, but knowing the signs that will tell you if there is something hidden inside that is valuable is even better. You may only get a few seconds to look, and you may only be able to see whatever you can see with your flashlight, it can be enough to decide if a unit is worth the risk or not.

From a reselling standpoint, you have lots of options. You can resell online, using places like eBay and Craigslist, or you can sell in person at yard sales or flea markets. Or you can use a middle man, like a pawn shop or an auction house. The more experience you have, the more you will get comfortable knowing where you should be selling your goods.

If you are interested in trying out the business, the single most important piece of advice is to attend an auction, even if you don't intend to win. Watch how the process works, look for the cues we mention in the book, and learn who the local players are. In this business, not only is knowledge power, it is the source of all power (other than cash.) It's highly advisable to attend a few auctions before you try bidding on anything.

Finally, know that this is a business. You need to commit your time and effort into making it work. You shouldn't expect to spend a few hours on it a month, and earn significant money. Learning what to buy, where to buy it, and how much to pay takes experience. Learning where to sell likewise takes some trial and error. And if you watch the professionals, they buy many units, knowing that the more you buy, the more likely you are to find a unit that makes a decent profit. The pros don't mind breaking even every now and again, because they know the next unit is right around the corner. Patience, persistence and experience will pay off in the end.

Made in the USA
Lexington, KY
02 April 2012